Temple Did It, and I Can, Too!

Nine Simple Life Rules

Introduction by Dr. Temple Grandin

by Jennifer Gilpin Yacio
Illustrated by Lynda Farrington Wilson

Temple Did It, and I Can, Too!
Nine Simple Life Rules

All marketing and publishing rights guaranteed to and reserved by:

© 2025 Jennifer Gilpin Yacio

Illustrated by Lynda Farrington Wilson

Layout by John Yacio III

ISBN: 978-1-963367-21-8

For Alex

Introduction by Dr. Temple Grandin

Nine of my life rules are listed in this book, but I consider one to be the most important: Work hard.

Creativity was always essential to me, but I had to work to achieve my goals. When I was a little girl, my mother and teachers always encouraged me to do my very best. There was always plenty of time for creativity, and my ability in art was supported. I spent hours outdoors, and I figured out how to fly small, paper bird kites behind my bike. I tried many designs until I made one that really flew well. Endless creative play outside taught me to keep trying a new way to make it. My mother encouraged me, but she never made the pictures or kite for me. She wanted me to figure it out by myself.

Hard work was always a necessity in my house. When I was only thirteen years old, Mother got me a sewing job and then when I went to boarding school, I cleaned eight horse stalls every day. This taught me discipline and responsibility as well as the pride of doing a good job. It also helped my self-esteem because I received recognition when I did a good art project and other people valued my work in the barn.

To all the children who will read this—Work hard and achieve your dreams.

May this book remind you to always do your very best and to develop your abilities.

— Dr. Temple Grandin

Throughout this story, the narrator's words will look like this.

And Temple's words will look like this.

Temple Grandin is a very successful scientist. She designs cattle systems and is famous for her advances in animal science. People come from miles around to hear her talk. They even made a movie about her. She is successful and famous.

But she wasn't always this way.

When she was a little girl, she couldn't talk.

2

When she was in school,
kids made fun of her.

3

I went to hear her talk one day and got to speak with her. I asked how she came so far.

These are the nine rules for success she taught me.

5

1. Follow your passion, and learn it well. My passion was cattle, so I learned everything about them.

2. Don't spend too much time playing video games or following pointless pursuits.

Live life! Spend your time studying,
and join clubs that interest you.
You'll be glad you did.

9

10

3. Be yourself, but you have to fit in a little. I never cared much for looking fancy, but I learned that people in business don't want to be around someone who is messy.

Now, I make sure to keep myself neat and clean and always have good manners.

But I still keep my own style.

4. Honesty is important, but you also have to be kind.

One day I was working in construction and told a welder that his welding work looked like pigeon poop.

12

My boss called me into his office and calmly explained that I should be honest but also be kind.

He said that otherwise I would never get my point across and might hurt someone's feelings. He said I should apologize to the welder and be more careful with my words. I did apologize, and—since then—I have been more thoughtful about what I say.

5. Always be present.

When you are talking to someone, pay attention to *them*. When you are working on a project, focus on *that*. Do not be on your phone or distracted. Everyone deserves your respect and full attention.

14

I thought about it and realized that Temple, with everything she has to do in the world, was focused only on me. That made me feel special. I need to remember to do this more often.

$-40 = 563 \sim n$

6. Develop your talent. Figure out what you can do with your favorite skills, and then practice and develop those skills. I like animals, so learned how to help them.

Hmm. I like math and bugs, so maybe one day I can become a computer programmer and design programs about insects!

166

$9a \times 4 = 5a - 2$

17

7. Perfection is not possible. Be good—not perfect.
Learn from your mistakes, and do your best.

18

8. Work hard.

Did you know that Temple didn't start out designing for animals; she started by cleaning horse stalls?

She spent three years doing this before she moved up to more interesting jobs, and it earned the respect of everyone around her.

19

9. Never stop learning. There is always something new to discover in your area of interest. Find your next goal.

FOLLOW PASSION. ☑
LIVE LIFE! ☑
BE YOURSELF. ☑
DEVELOP YOUR TALENTS. ☑
NEVER STOP LEARNING. ☑
PERFECT IS NOT POSSIBLE. ☑
WORK HARD.

Temple followed her rules, and now she is famous and influential in not one, but two fields, animal behavior and autism!

22

Temple Grandin did this, and she had more to overcome than I do.

So if I try hard and spend time developing my talents into something good, someday I will succeed, too.

23

Workbook Pages

Everyone, Every Day

Temple's rules are general life rules and apply to everyone, every day. Let's look closer at them.

1. Follow your passion, and learn everything you can about it.

Whatever it is! Maybe your passion today is insects, maybe it is trains. Whatever you are interested in, learn more!

2. Live life.

Yes, yes, yes. Go out and enjoy the world. Everyone needs alone time with books or video games, but you get so much more when you experience life, too.

3. Be yourself, but you have to fit in a little.

This is true for all of us! There are some social rules you should follow, and you should always have good manners. But, you can still be your unique self.

4. Honesty is important.

Yes! It is so important to be honest and straightforward when interacting with others. But it is also important to balance honesty with *tact* in certain situations. If something you say might hurt someone's feelings or make them feel bad about themselves, think of another way to say what you need to say.

5. Always be present.

This can be a tough one for all of us. There are so many distractions in todays world, especially screens, which always show us something new. But being there for your friends and family is more important. It's good to practice enjoying conversation with them, and you will always have time for doing something on your own later!

6. Develop your talents.

What is your favorite talent? If you do not know, you can try a few things that might interest you, and find out what you enjoy. Then you can develop that talent by practicing and honing your skills.

7. Perfect is not possible.

This is important for all of us to understand. We would love to be perfect, and should *aim* for perfection on projects or goals, but be okay if everything doesn't go just right. Every mistake is a chance for you to learn what not to do next time. It's okay. Giving 100% is something you control, and you can be pleased with yourself when you know you gave your all, even if the results aren't perfect!

8. Work hard.

The harder you work, the closer you get to reaching your goals. And, you feel better about yourself when you've done your best, too!

9. Never stop learning.

This is true for everyone! There is always something new to learn and experience in the world, whether it is for your life's passion, or just something that interests you.

Do you have a goal you can use Temple's guidelines on? Try it!

1. Follow your passion.

My passions include: _____

My favorite interest is: _____

2. Live life.

One group I would like to join is: _____

One activity I would like to do outside the house is: _____

3. Be yourself.

One way I am different than my friends is: _____

4. KIND honesty is important.

Name one time when you had to be honest about something but didn't want to hurt someones feelings. How could you do that differently today?

_____

_____

5. Always be present.

How can I start being more present in everyday life? _____

_____

6. Develop your talents.

Some of my talents are: (It's okay if your talents are the same as your passions.) _____

_____

My favorite talent is: _____

7. Perfect is not possible.

One time when I was upset that I was not perfect was: _____

NOW, I would react differently. I would: _____

8. Work hard.

One way I can work hard at my talent or passion is to: _____

9. Never stop learning.

My next step in learning is to: _____

About the Creators

About the Inspiration

photo ©
Rosalie Winard

Dr. Temple Grandin's insights into animal behavior and her innovations in livestock handling have revolutionized food-animal welfare. Along the way, Dr. Grandin has also inspired people around the world as a champion for individuals with autism and their families. Her accomplishments as a speaker, author, and advocate earned her a place among *Time Magazine*'s 100 Most Influential People in 2010, and her life story was the subject of the acclaimed 2010 HBO biopic *Temple Grandin*, winner of seven Emmy Awards and a Golden Globe. Temple is world-famous for using insights gained from her autism to lead dramatic improvements in the livestock industry. A professor at Colorado State University for more than thirty years, she is a celebrated speaker who lectures internationally on autism and livestock handling.

About the Author

Jennifer Gilpin Yacio is the president of Future Horizons and Sensory World. Ever since her little brother was diagnosed with autism in 1982, she has been interested in both autism and how people are affected by their senses. With an extensive career in both the publishing and autism fields, the leap to heading a company solely for understanding autism and the senses was an easy one.

Jennifer is happy to be updating *Temple Did It, and I Can, Too!*, her first children's book, as being an author has been a long-time dream.

About the Illustrator

Lynda Farrington Wilson is a beloved children's book author and illustrator, as well as a passionate advocate for autism awareness. She has authored five books and illustrated over 120 thus far. Endorsed by Dr. Temple Grandin, her award-winning book titled *Squirmy Wormy, How I Learned to Help Myself* was written for her youngest son, a sensory-seeker with autism. Lynda has 3 sons and 6 grandchildren. She works out of her Lime Crab Cottage studio in Smith Mountain Lake, VA. You can see her work at www.lyndafarringtonwilson.com.

Also by Lynda Farrington Wilson

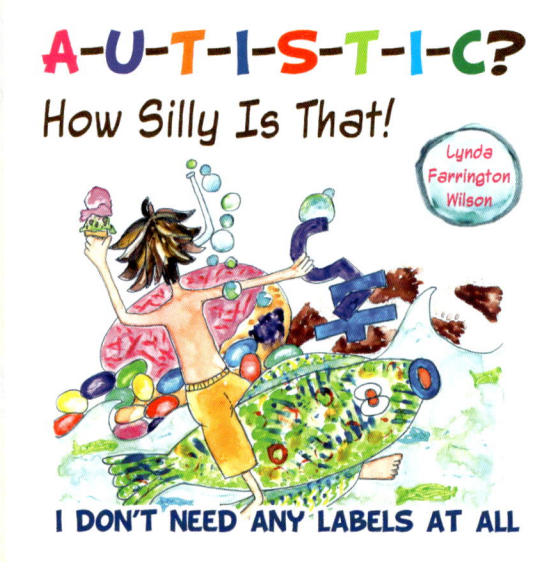

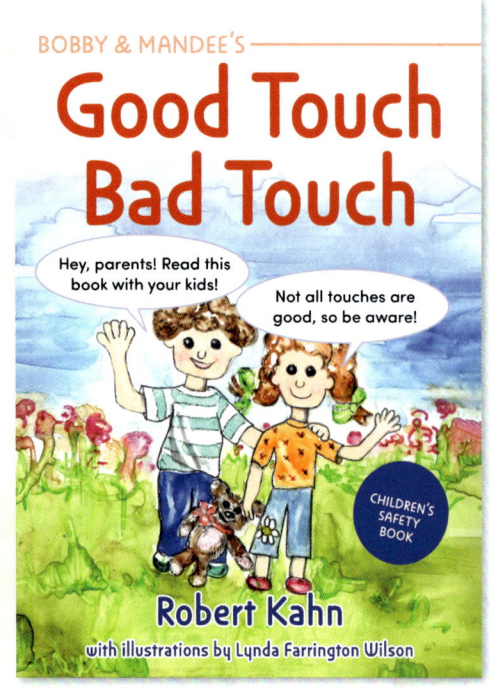

As illustrator

 www.FHautism.com | 817.277.0727